THANKSGIVING

by Robin Nelson

first step nonfiction

Lerner Publications Company · Minneapolis

We celebrate Thanksgiving
every year.

2009 November

SUNDAY	MONDAY	TUESDAY	WEDNESDAY	THURSDAY	FRIDAY	SATURDAY
1	2	3	4	5	6	7
8	9	10	11	12	13	14
15	16	17	18	19	20	21
22	23	24	25	26 Thanksgiving	27	28
29	30					

This holiday is on the fourth Thursday of November.

Long ago, **colonists** came
to America.

They met people called the
Wampanoag.

The Wampanoag already
lived and hunted in the area.

The colonists and Wampanoag lived in **peace**.

In the fall, the colonists
celebrated their fall **harvest**.

The Wampanoag and colonists brought food to the **feast**.

Together they gave thanks
for the food.

They ate deer and wild bird
meat.

They ate the crops they
grew like corn and pumpkin.

It was a great Thanksgiving feast.

We celebrate Thanksgiving
with our families.

We eat turkey, potatoes, cranberries, and pie.

We watch parades.

We give thanks for all that we have.

Thanksgiving Timeline

1621
English colonists and the Wampanoag had the first Thanksgiving.

1789
President George Washington proclaimed November 26, 1789, to be a day of thanksgiving.

1863
President
Abraham Lincoln
proclaimed
Thanksgiving
a holiday.

November 26,1941
President
Franklin Roosevelt
made Thanksgiving the
fourth Thursday in
November.

Thanksgiving Facts

 The colonists are sometimes called pilgrims.

 How do you say Wampanoag? Wam-pah-NO-ag.

 The first Thanksgiving was actually in October.

 The first Thanksgiving was three days long.

 There were 52 colonists and 90 Wampanoag people at the Thanksgiving feast.

The largest pumpkin pie ever baked weighed 2,020 pounds and measured just over 12 feet long.

 The first Macy's Thanksgiving Day Parade took place in New York City in 1924.

 Canada's Thanksgiving is held on the second Monday in October.

Glossary

colonists – people who settle in a new land. The colonists at the first Thanksgiving came to America from England.

feast – a big meal

harvest – gathering crops

peace – without war

Wampanoag – a group of native people in America

Index

The images in this book are used with the permission of: © Ariel Skelley/Photographer's Choice/ Getty Images, pp. 2, 14; © Independent Picture Service, p. 3; © North Wind Picture Archives, pp. 4, 5, 7, 10, 22 (1st, 4th and 5th from top); Private Collection/Photo © Christie's Images/ The Bridgeman Art Library, p. 6; The Granger Collection, New York, pp. 8, 11, 22 (3rd from top); Everett Collection, pp. 9, 22 (2nd from top); © Bettmann/CORBIS, p. 12; © Marilyn Angel Wynn/Nativestock.com, p. 13; © Stockbyte/Getty Images, p. 15; © Richey Miller/Cal Sport Media/ZUMA Press, p. 16; © Yellow Dog Productions/Stone/Getty Images, p. 17. Cover: © Hiroko Masuike/Getty Images.

Lerner Publications Company
A division of Lerner Publishing Group, Inc.
241 First Avenue North
Minneapolis, MN 55401 U.S.A.

Website address: www.lernerbooks.com

Library of Congress Cataloging-in-Publication Data

Nelson, Robin, 1971–
    Thanksgiving / by Robin Nelson.
        p.   cm. — (First step nonfiction. American holidays)
    Includes index.
    ISBN 978–0–7613–4901–3 (lib. bdg. : alk. paper)
    1. Thanksgiving Day—Juvenile literature. I. Title.
GT4975.N456 2010
394.2649—dc22   2009010548

Manufactured in the United States of America
1 2 3 4 5 6 – DP – 15 14 13 12 11 10